D0442194

Sharing Silence

Also by Gunilla Norris

Being Home: A Book of Meditations 1991

Becoming Bread: Meditations on Loving and Transformation 1993

Sharing Silence

Meditation Practice and Mindful Living

Gunilla Norris

BELL TOWER/NEW YORK

Published by Bell Tower, an imprint of Harmony Books, a division of Crown Publishers, Inc., 201 East 50th Street, New York, New York 10022. Member of the Crown Publishing Group.

Random House, Inc. New York, Toronto, London, Sydney, Auckland

Originally published in a limited edition as *Shared Silence* by Small Offerings Press, Newtown, Connecticut, in 1992.

Manufactured in the United States of America

Library of Congress Cataloging-in-Publication Data

Norris, Gunilla Brodde

Sharing silence : meditation practice and mindful living / Gunilla Norris. — 1st Bell Tower ed.

p. cm.

1. Meditation. 2. Spiritual life. 3. Silence—Religious aspects.

I. Title.

BL627.N66 1993

291.4′3—dc20 92-44971 CIP

ISBN 0-517-59506-0

10 9 8 7 6 5 4 3 2 1

First Bell Tower Edition

Contents

Foreword

Within each of us there is a silence
—a silence as vast as the universe.
We are afraid of it . . . and we long for it.

When we experience that silence, we remember
who we are; creatures of the stars, created
from the birth of galaxies, created
from the cooling of this planet, created
from dust and gas, created
from the elements, created
from time and space . . . created
from silence.

Silence is the source of all that exists,
the unfathomable stillness where vibration began
—the first oscillation, the first word,
from which life emerged. Silence is our deepest nature,
our home, our common ground, our peace.
Silence reveals. Silence heals.

Silence is where God dwells.
We yearn to be there. We yearn to share it.

And yet, in our present culture,
silence is something like an endangered species . . .
an endangered fundamental.
The experience of silence is now so rare
that we must guard it and treasure it.
This is especially true for shared silence.

Sharing silence with others is a political act.
Silence brings us back to basics, to our senses,
to our selves. It locates us. Without that return
we can go so far away from our true natures
that we end up, quite literally,
beside ourselves. We live blindly and act thoughtlessly.
We endanger the delicate balance which sustains
our lives, our communities, and our planet.

I believe that each of us can make a tremendous
difference. Politicians and visionaries will not
return us to the sacredness of life.
That will be done by ordinary men and women

who gather neighbors and friends together and say,
"Remember to breathe, remember to feel, remember to care,
remember life. Let us do this together
for ourselves and our children
and our children's children."

In this book I want to share some thoughts
about silence. I want to invite you, my neighbor,
to remember your power as a person.
I want to remind myself and others
that our homes can become sacred spaces,
filled with life and meaning.
We do not need to be experts or gurus or geniuses
to remember that all of existence is precious.
We do not need cathedrals to remind ourselves
to experience the sacred. We need only be
deeply respectful of what is fundamentally true.
And that is what we rediscover when we join in silence.

This little book, then, is offered to those
who have begun or are beginning the practice
of contemplation in silence.

It is for spiritual friends to use with each other
or separately. It is for any group of people
who have made a commitment to sit together.*

There are many traditions from both East and West
that teach meditation, concentration, centering,
and devotional methods. All of them are anchored
in mindfulness and silence. This primer is
a reminder of some essential attitudes and principles
which can be helpful in any meditation practice.
It is a simple tool for anyone of any tradition to use,
and is offered with reverence for all who honor
and use silence as a way.

** If you are unfamiliar with the basic concepts and procedures of group meditation, you may wish to refer to the Afterword beginning on page 51 to get your bearings.*

Room

When we make a place for silence, we make room
for ourselves. This is simple. And it is radical.
A room set apart for silence becomes a sanctuary
—a place for breath, for refreshment, for challenge,
and for healing. It is helpful to keep the space plain
and simple: a few cushions, a rug . . .
Simplicity allows the senses to rest from stimulation.

Silent spaces invite us to go to the inner room
—the room inside ourselves.
By making room for silence, we resist
the forces of the world which tell us to live
an advertised life of surface appearances,
instead of a discovered life—a life lived in contact
with our senses, our feelings, our deepest thoughts and values.

When a space is reserved solely for mindfulness practice,
the silence seems to deepen. A room devoted to silence
honors and invites the unknown, the untamed, the wild,

the shy, the unfathomable
—that which rarely has a chance to surface
within us. It is a visible, external symbol
of an internal reality: An actual room
signifying space within ourselves
set aside for silence.

Preparation

Before we eat a meal, we purchase food and prepare it.
Before we go on a journey, we assemble and pack
the things we need. Any activity requires preparation.
This is true for a time of silence as well.

We need a place to practice silence,
and we also need an atmosphere—a sense of harmony,
an ambiance of quiet beauty to help us on the way.

We can arrange a vase of flowers or simple greens
to soothe our eyes and help us recall
that we are part of nature, part of the order of things.

We can light a candle to ease our passage
into a different mode of being.
Perhaps it will remind us that we have inner light
to discover and share.

We can burn a stick of incense
to mark time, as Buddhist monks do:
a short stick for a half-hour of sitting,
a longer stick for forty-five minutes . . .
aromatic time. Odor reminds us
that we are sensate creatures,
that our souls live in and through our bodies.

We can strike a bell at the start of a period of sitting.
We can let the sound ring into us
—let it sound us, as in navigation, to find our depth.

Preparations like these help us to be more present
on the journey into our selves, into the world
we share in silence.

Time

A group that sits needs a time to begin
—and everyone must agree to be on time.
Starting a period of silence
and having it broken by someone's late arrival
is like the shattering of a glass.
The silence must be recovered bit by bit
and then reassembled. This takes effort.
And everyone must do it—not just the one who was late.

It is not so easy to be punctual, but it is important.
The discipline is a self-courtesy.
It teaches us to value ourselves, each other,
and the time we have been given.

To be on time we need to experience ourselves in time.
Our inner lives are timeless,
and yet our days are numbered.
To work with time we need a sense of leisure,
a sense of the natural unfolding of a day,

of a season, a year, a life.
We need also to be present to our experiences,
moment to moment. This makes for timeliness.
Then we can feel the rhythm of our lives.
Our timing becomes finer and finer.
We do not miss a beat. Leisurely and precise,
we can flow with time.

It is also helpful to allow time for the silence
to reverberate after a period of sitting.
When we are deeply touched we need time to feel.
We can dissipate what we have gained by talking
or by moving on to the next thing too quickly.
After a performance of music, there is often a quiet moment
before the audience breaks into applause. So, too,
after a period of deep sitting: Moments of quiet rest
together help us integrate what we have experienced,
easing the transition from stillness to activity.

Presence

We cannot really experience anything without being
present to it. True presence requires that we be attentive
to what is happening . . . here and now. It is an offering
of our awareness, our participation, and our willingness.
This is a basic and profound courtesy.
By such courtesy we are deeply transformed.

In silence we discover ourselves, our actual presence
to the life in us and around us. When we are present,
deeply attentive, we cannot be busy controlling.
Instead we become beholders—giving ourselves up
to the mystery of things. We become more willing
to let things be. And, as a consequence,
we can also let ourselves be.

This is so simple . . . and so hard.
Many of us have become uncomfortable with silence.
We do not regard it as a friend. In its presence
we feel uneasy, out of control.

We seek superficial reassurance for our busy minds,
instead of the deep confidence offered by
our silent vitality.

It takes time to rediscover the treasure of silence.
In it we can be found again. But we learn this
only by learning. By being present, moment to moment,
we may discern the richness of silence in ourselves
and in each other.

Sharing silence with others is a profound act of trust,
love, and courtesy. It is a mutual gift, a necessity,
a helping hand, a path, and a discipline.

Through silence our days are illumined—like rooms
filled with light—so we may inhabit our lives.

Bearing

When we sit in mindfulness practice
our backs should be straight.
Our upright posture took millions of years
to evolve. This gives our bodies an inherent dignity.

When we are upright in body we tend to be present
and alert in spirit as well. Energy can travel freely
along the spine, dancing up to the crown of the head
and down to the sacrum.

Crown and sacrum. These words hint at our worth.
When our bearing has dignity we acknowledge
the royal and sacred nature of our true selves.

Relationship

To become ourselves we need others.
Only in and through relationship do we truly become
persons. We know this from childhood.
We first learn of our existence through the eyes
of our parents. They are our first mirrors.
The process of learning who we are
—and who we might become—continues
through all the relationships of our lives.
In the deep resonance of companionship
we dare to journey to the center.

It is important to recognize how much we need
each other. This recognition removes the illusion
that we are self-created. It teaches us that giving
and taking are like inhaling and exhaling
—the breath of relationship.
By recognizing our need for each other we acknowledge
that every aspect of reality is connected to the whole,
that nothing is separate from us.

Sharing silence with another creates a bond
that cannot be compared to ordinary exchanges.
It helps us know that each of us is essential;
a vibrating essence. When we sit quietly together,
we can sense that vibration. We can feel it
singing in our cells.

When we speak, when we act, when we offer each other
food and water, we give form and expression
to the essential vibration within us. We become,
in a sense, living words. Words in combination
make complete, meaningful phrases.
Through this collaboration, potentials can be realized.
Worlds are created. In the language of life,
we are words of power.

When we support the silence in one another,
we discover what we each have been given to be.
The silence in each of us is the medium
through which the words we are may be spoken,
clearly and purely. In silence we are revealed.
This is universal and very personal.

Practice

Walking, eating a meal, dancing, breathing, chanting—
anything can be a practice as long as we are mindful,
as long as we are fully present. There are many ways,
many traditions.

To bring silence into our bodies and minds,
we must learn to be quiet. We begin by being still.
If a period of physical stillness is all we can muster,
that is enough. We have begun to practice.

If we can learn simply to follow our breath
in a steady way—attending to the inhalation
and the exhalation until we feel that we are
no longer breathing, but are being breathed
—we have grown in practice.

The point of practice is not to perform,
but to participate—not to achieve specific experiences,
but to develop a new relationship to experience itself.

When we no longer need to know
(or need to understand, or need to be something
other than what we are)—we are free.
We can then experience the pure unfolding of life,
the rapture of truly living. This makes happiness possible.

From the deep well of silence, joy is constantly bubbling
up and flowing out. Practice reveals that we are
immersed in that joy. Practice also reveals
what is blocking the flow.

Mutuality

When we form a group for sharing silence
it is helpful to share the leadership as well.
If only one person leads, others may become lazy,
resentful, or bored. By taking turns, we acknowledge
that all of us make up the whole.
Our responsibility is mutual. We all respond
(which originally meant to "pledge back")
by giving and receiving equitably.

When we form a group for sharing silence,
commitment to it is essential.
Our promise to each other is that we will be present
to ourselves and therefore to one another.
Together we make a holding place, much like the stones
in a well: Side by side, they make a containment
for the living water to rise through the ground,
so that anyone can draw from it.

There is no well if the stones are not steady.
As in all deep things, constancy is necessary.
Through it we become sturdy, reliable, and trustworthy,
and so find our ground water.

Mutuality and commitment—in life as in sitting,
we must give of ourselves in order to receive.

Methods

A few basic methods are helpful
in any mindfulness practice:
The first is to have a precise intention.
By focusing on one objective during a period
of meditation, we grow in concentration.

We may choose to follow our breath,
note our body's sensations, or track
the sequence of our thoughts. The objective itself
is not as important as staying with it.

The second is to be allowing—giving ourselves
to whatever comes up in the mind in relation
to our chosen objective. If we are spacious
and open-hearted to the internal flow of events,
the habitual ways in which we congeal against experience
will be broken down, releasing us into new life.

The third is to be steadfast. In returning to the practice
over and over, whether we feel like it or not, we gain
composure—no matter what
kind of experience we are having.

The fourth is to be accepting of the fact
that we cannot be flawless in our practice.
We can do what we can do.
We can be relatively still, relatively focused,
relatively allowing. Our capacity is different
in every period of silence. No matter what
our daily practice is like, however,
there is a noticeable gain over time.
If we are open to this process,
we may derive a deep sense of satisfaction
from the knowledge that we are engaged
in something larger than ourselves.
We are contacting our source.

Rhythm

Learning to be measured, to be steady in our pace,
is a process that must take place in the body.
When we strive to do things we are learning strife.
When we strain we are learning strain.
We must learn to move rhythmically, easily,
to be un-driven, to flow.

Study the way waves wash onto the shore,
or the way rings float out on a lake
when a pebble splashes through the surface
—moving without apparent effort. There is
an organic pace to this. We, too, have an organic rhythm.
Silence can help us feel it.

When we sit quietly we will sense
how long an interval of sitting is right for us.
When we practice steadily we will also know
how often to return to silence in any given day.

In our culture we do not trust time. We try to defy time.
We steal time, kill time. We want to control
the flow of events, instead of trusting
in a natural rhythm—instead of trusting
that we can and will meet life as it happens.

We attack life to defend against the mistrust
we have of ourselves. In silence we can learn
to change this. We can give ourselves time,
leaning into it, resting in it. When we do this,
the pressure comes off and we give ourselves permission
to feel and experience—because we are participating
in our lives, not controlling them. Then,
like still ponds at early dawn, we reflect
effortless effort.

Suffering

Through the practice of silence we become aware
of our pain. The pain is always there—in our minds
and in our bodies. Silence allows us to see it,
face it, release it.

We constantly judge ourselves. Our minds decide
what our experience should or should not be
—relentlessly labeling things good or bad—
and demand that our lives conform to our labels.
Then, when pain comes into our lives
—and it does to every life—we not only suffer it,
but we suffer our suffering as well.
We add the mind's harsh judgment of pain
to our actual experience of it.

By practicing silence, we may discover the ways
in which we intensify our pain by judging it.
Then we have a chance to become less harsh,
more forgiving.

The pain created by our minds is stored in our bodies,
creating rigid patterns of behavior, blocking the flow
of energy within us, cramping our being.
Our harshness and our fears are embodied in our flesh.
In silence, we can feel these tendencies harden—
and allow them to be as they are. They may then
uncramp and release, for anything that is not resisted
tends of its own accord to unfold and change.

By cultivating silence, we can find and release
deeper and deeper levels of pain and so discover
once again what is beneath the pain:
the natural joy that is already inside us,
free to rise and flow into experience.

Tendencies

The fears in our unconscious minds
create particular ways of defending
against full participation in our lives.
For whatever reason, we are each
predisposed to act and respond in certain ways.

By looking closely at these tendencies as we sit,
we may learn a great deal about ourselves.
Perhaps we will encounter chronic sleepiness,
discovering that we lack the energy
to remain awake and attentive.
Looking deeply we may find
that in our childhood we did not receive
enough attention, enough engagement,
and learned to sleep through the pain of neglect.
In silence we may slowly learn
to value and participate with ourselves.

We may find that we are measuring ourselves
against others, comparing and monitoring. Looking
deeply into childhood, we may discover
that we were asked to perform, instead of being enjoyed.
Perhaps we never had a chance to know
the pleasurable people we are. In silence
we can let this go and feel our incomparable selves.

We may feel chronic anger rising up, a hot gall.
Perhaps we were not fully heard when we were young.
We may have been shamed, or treated unjustly.
Our natural rhythms of behavior, self-discovery,
or expression may have been broken in some way,
leaving a residue of frustration in our bodies.
In silence we can learn to hear our forgotten selves,
to feel and to respond to the deep levels of our identity
that are surfacing at last.

We may discover a tremendous greed, old feelings
of having been cheated, overlooked, and dismissed.
We may actually feel the automatic impulses which are
the beginnings of our compensation for such feelings

—the compulsions that lead to overeating,
overworking, drinking, excessive sexual activity.
These compensations are meant to soothe,
to remind ourselves that we exist, but ultimately
they hurt us. In silence we can learn much about this.

We may come to realize that our habitual doubt
is a mask for self-deprecation—an unwillingness
to acknowledge what we have and what we are.
We may find that our boredom is simple laziness
—a refusal to pay attention. We may see
that our discouragement is based on false ideas
of entitlement. We think we are owed when we are not.
The lessons of silence are myriad.

In silence we have the common goal to honor
and protect our spirits. We are not being diagnostic
or prescriptive with one another. We are making
profound room in ourselves—for ourselves and
for each other. Then our tendencies can come up
as they will, one by one, and we can smile at them.
We can suffer them directly. We can slowly learn

to accept what cannot be changed . . .

and what is already whole and good within us.

In the grace of shared silence we can know

that we are imperfect and complete.

Paradox

It is a paradox that we encounter so much internal noise
when we first try to sit in silence.

It is a paradox that experiencing pain releases pain.

It is a paradox that keeping still can lead us
so fully into life and being.

Our minds do not like paradoxes. We want things
to be clear, so we can maintain our illusions of safety.
Certainty breeds tremendous smugness.

We each possess a deeper level of being, however,
which loves paradox. It knows that summer is already
growing like a seed in the depth of winter. It knows
that the moment we are born, we begin to die. It knows
that all of life shimmers, in shades of becoming
—that shadow and light are always together,
the visible mingled with the invisible.

When we sit in stillness we are profoundly active.
Keeping silent, we can hear the roar of existence.
Through our willingness to be the one we are,
we become one with everything.

Steadfastness

How do we sustain the courage and the will
to continue our practice when the going gets rough?
We know it will get rough,
and that we will encounter weariness,
frustration, and doubt.

Practicing mindfulness is much like physical training.
The long-distance runner must deal with hills
as well as valleys. The hills are hard.
And they make one strong.
If we can welcome them, and know
that they will be followed by valleys,
we will be learning something about steadfastness.

We may find the strength to continue
by taking the long view: recognizing that bliss and pain
are part of each other, that both together are more
than either is separately. Together they form reality,
the only thing that truly satisfies us.

Alternatively, we may look closely enough to see
that perseverance is also a matter of valuing
what is happening now—for its own sake.
Moment to moment, we continue by engaging fully
in the rich, dense, prolific dance of life.

Taking the long view and looking closely . . .
background and foreground.
By perseverance—through perseverance—
we become steadfast and sturdy.
We become present.

Phenomena

As we sit, we may experience many different sensations:
Our bodies may become very warm or very cold.
Our skin may become prickly and uncomfortable.
There may be a melting feeling, as if liquid gold
were coursing through us. We may see beautiful colors,
smell unusual odors. We may hear the body/mind
get stuck in old conversations, or repeating
tunes from the hit parade.

These phenomena are not of much importance.
They are not to be hungered after
or assiduously avoided. They just happen
as the body and mind begin to release
the accumulated tensions of experience.

Any phenomenon may be selected
as the object of concentration.
When one becomes especially dominant,
we have little choice but to make it our focus.

As we do this, we may discover that the phenomena
we find so compelling are not static,
but continually changing and moving and passing
on to something else.

Bit by bit, we may learn to see that everything
is impermanent, always rising or falling. We may learn
that all phenomena rest on something deeper;
something vast, endless, and timeless—our source.

Individuality

We are not static beings, and yet we are called to be
exactly who we are, unique individuals.
Our specific genetic code,
our parental influence, our education,
our friends, our work,
our whole history of experiences
—these are all the particulars through which
we have become who we are now.

When we truly acknowledge and embrace
these particulars we are making a profound contribution.
We are consciously accepting our limits,
even as they continue to change.
This is both solemn and joyful. It is what we,
as conscious beings, are asked to do—to accept
our small and unique places in this universe.

Just as water is the natural element of a fish,
our element is the vastness of life.

A fish can know water only by living in it,
swimming in it, and drawing it in through its gills.
A fish cannot know water except as a fish.
So, too, with us. We can know our true place,
our purpose, and our source only through our humanity
—by experiencing the vastness that is moving
through our small individuality. Then we will feel
intimately known, trusted, and upheld.

Passion

Because passion is an expression of love,
it encompasses suffering as well.
Love and suffering are always intertwined.

When we suffer what is truly ours to suffer, we move
into union with ourselves. We want this experience
of love, and we are afraid of it.

On some level, we know that the true meaning
of suffering is found in allowing each moment to be
what it is, remaining open to the vastness
—the life—that wants to move through us.
Where, but in silence, can we be present enough
to witness that urge of life within?

We discover these depths through silence, stillness,
and the simple act of being attentive with others.

As we enter into exquisite awareness of the life
that wants to live *as us,* we learn to love deeply.
We claim our passion.

Peace

Peace is not absence of strife. Peace is acceptance
and surrender to that which is. Peace is
the profound awareness of the one true source
from which all things emerge . . .
and to which all things return.

However lost we may feel, we are never outside
of the source. We are intimately known by it,
sustained by it, and returned to it—daily . . . now . . .
and when we pass away. The source delights in us,
becomes in us, plays in us.

When we contact the source, our practice
has led us to the end and to the beginning.
Then we can be at peace—for no matter what occurs
in our lives, we can always find our way home
to the core, the truth of our being.

Afterword

There are countless ways of sharing silence with others: daily practice, weekly practice, longer retreats . . . sitting with friends, family, or more formally organized groups . . . simply sitting in silence, with no structure at all . . . working with images, with sound, with movement . . . employing any of the various forms of mindfulness practice, which may involve all of our senses, our thinking and feeling. Many books are readily available from which you may learn more about any of these approaches.

The basic procedures of a period of meditation (or a *sit*) are wonderfully simple: Select a room. Put some cushions on the floor. Sit on them. Each period of sitting may last from thirty minutes to an hour or more. A single period of perhaps forty-five minutes, once a week, is a good first goal (though you may wish to begin with thirty minutes until everyone can comfortably sit for longer periods).

Later you may wish to move on to occasional all-day sits, consisting of five or more sessions of varying lengths, with ten-minute "intermissions," an hour for lunch (ideally without conversation), and one or two "walking meditations" (in which one person leads the others on a slow and mindful walk, in silence, indoors or out). The groups which inspired this book have chosen to sit once a week for an hour and once a month for a day. The sits are always held in the same room, which is not used for any other purpose. Generally the leadership is shared.

As a discipline, we select a topic which will be our focus of contemplation over the course of several months. These topics are always "large" and simple, such as *trust, simplicity, compassion, or community.*

Our periods of silence often begin with a few minutes of spoken reflection by that day's leader. Though group leaders are encouraged to speak in their own words, some prefer not to. In that case, there are many excellent books from which to read aloud. Here are a few favorites:

Tao Te Ching: A New English Version with Foreword and Notes by Stephen Mitchell (HarperCollins).

The poems of the Sufi mystic, Rumi, translated by John Moyne and Coleman Barks. Some titles are: *These Branching Moments* (Copper Beech Press), *We Are Three* (Maypop Books), *Open Secret* and *Unseen Rain* (Threshold Books).

Zen Mind, Beginner's Mind by Shunryu Suzuki, (Weatherhill).

The Miracle of Mindfulness (Beacon Press) and *Being Peace* (Parallax Press) by Thich Nhat Hanh.

One might ask: Why read or speak at all if the point is to be together in silence? My answer would be that words can both grow out of silence and bring us to it. The discursive, conceptual mind is always at work. By giving it something to work with, we allow our non-conceptual mind—the *being* part of us—to sink deep into the well of silence and breathe the mystery of what always is and can never be named.

After the leader has spoken, a bell is rung to signify the start of silence and the beginning of meditation. How we sit is a private matter: Some of us close our eyes, some keep them open but unfocused. Though sitting cross-legged and straight-backed is recommended, some of us prefer to sit with legs outstretched or to use a kneeling bench. At the designated time, with some allowance for an intuitive sense of the right moment, the bell is rung again to conclude the sit. After resting quietly for a short while, we share whatever thoughts and impressions we wish to pass along to each other.

Mindfulness practice is greatly enriched by the discipline of sustaining concentration for extended periods—a whole day, a week, a month. A good resource book to help structure such experiences is *Silence, Simplicity and Solitude: A Guide for Spiritual Retreat* by David A. Cooper (Bell Tower). It has a fine overview of the major spiritual traditions and a good bibliography, as well as sample schedules for days of meditative retreat.

If a sitting group remains stable through months and years, deep communion and trust grow, along with the capacity to dwell in silence for longer and longer periods of time. Through this process, we are fundamentally changed and begin to participate in the peace that lies beyond understanding.

Acknowledgments

My deep gratitude goes to Greta D. Sibley for the generous and unfailing attention she has given to this project and for her design of a limited edition of the book published by Small Offerings Press. In addition, I want to thank Norman Sibley for his superb editorial help in the limited edition publication of this book.

My appreciation to my editor at Bell Tower, Toinette Lippe, for her faithful encouragement and support.

And lastly, my gratitude to everyone who has deeply participated in the shared silences that inspired and sustained the writing of this book.

About the Author

Gunilla Norris lives in Mystic, Connecticut, where she works as a writer and psychotherapist in private practice. She is the author of *Being Home: A Book of Meditations* and *Becoming Bread: Meditations on Loving and Transformation*, eleven children's books, and one book of poems, *Learning from the Angel*.

Other Bell Tower Books

The pure sound of the bell
summons us into the present moment.
The timeless ring of truth is expressed
in many different voices, each one magnifying
and illuminating the sacred.
The clarity of its song resonates within us
and calls us away from those things
which often distract us—that which was, that which
might be—to That Which Is.

Being Home
A Book of Meditations
by Gunilla Norris
Photographs by Greta D. Sibley
An exquisite modern book of hours, a celebration of
mindfulness in everyday activities.
Hardcover 0-517-58159-0(1991)

Nourishing Wisdom
A New Understanding of Eating
by Marc David
A book that advocates awareness in eating and reveals
how our attitude to food reflects our attitude to life.
Hardcover 0-517-57636-8(1991)

Sanctuaries: The Northeast
A Guide to Lodgings in Monasteries, Abbeys, and Retreats
of the United States
by Jack and Marcia Kelly
The first in a series of regional guides for those
in search of renewal and a little peace.
Softcover 0-517-57727-5(1991)

Grace Unfolding

Psychotherapy in the Spirit of the Tao-te ching

by Greg Johanson and Ron Kurtz

The interaction of client and therapist illuminated through the gentle power and wisdom of Lao Tzu's ancient Chinese classic.

Hardcover 0-517-58449-2(1991)

Self-Reliance

The Wisdom of Ralph Waldo Emerson as Inspiration for Daily Living

Selected and with an introduction by Richard Whelan

A distillation of Emerson's essential spiritual writings for contemporary readers.

Softcover 0-517-58512-X(1991)

Compassion in Action

Setting Out on the Path of Service

By Ram Dass and Mirabai Bush

Heartfelt encouragement and advice for those ready to commit time and energy to relieving suffering in the world.

Softcover 0-517-57635-X(1992)

Letters from a Wild State

Rediscovering Our True Relationship to Nature

by James G. Cowan

A luminous interpretation of Aboriginal spiritual experience applied to the leading issue of our time: the care of the earth.

Hardcover 0-517-58770-X(1992)

Silence, Simplicity, and Solitude

A Guide for Spiritual Retreat

by David A. Cooper

This classic guide to meditation and other traditional spiritual practice is required reading for anyone contemplating a retreat.

Hardcover 0-517-58620-7(1992)

The Heart of Stillness

The Elements of Spiritual Practice

by David A. Cooper

A comprehensive guidebook to the basic principles of inner work—a companion volume to *Silence, Simplicity, and Solitude.*

Hardcover 0-517-58621-5(1992)

One Hundred Graces

Selected by Marcia and Jack Kelly

With calligraphy by Christopher Gausby

A collection of mealtime graces from many traditions, beautifully inscribed in calligraphy reminiscent of the manuscripts of medieval Europe.

Hardcover 0-517-58567-7(1992)

Sanctuaries: The West Coast and Southwest

A Guide to Lodgings in Monasteries, Abbeys, and Retreats of the United States

by Marcia and Jack Kelly

The second volume of what *The New York Times* called "the *Michelin Guide* of the retreat set."

Softcover 0-517-88007-5(1993)

Becoming Bread
Meditations on Loving and Transformation
by Gunilla Norris
A book linking the food of the spirit—love—
with the food of the body—bread.
Hardcover 0-517-59168-5(1993)

Messengers of the Gods
Tribal Elders Reveal the Ancient Wisdom of the Earth
A lyrical and visionary journey
through the metaphysical landscapes of
Northern Australia and the islands just beyond it.
Softcover 0-517-88078-4(1993)

Pilgrimage to Dzhvari
A Woman's Journey of Spiritual Awakening
by Valeria Alfeyeva
A powerful and eloquent account of a contemporary Russian
woman's discovery of her Christian heritage.
A modern *Way of a Pilgrim.*
Hardcover 0-517-59194-4(1993)

The Journal of Hildegard of Bingen
by Barbara Lachman
A liturgical year in the life of the 12th-century German mystic,
abbess, composer, and healer. This fictional diary is the one
she never had time to write herself.
Hardcover 0-517-59169-3(1993)